Cardinals

Leo Statts

abdopublishing.com

Published by Abdo Zoom™, PO Box 398166, Minneapolis, Minnesota 55439. Copyright © 2018 by Abdo Consulting Group, Inc. International copyrights reserved in all countries. No part of this book may be reproduced in any form without written permission from the publisher. Abdo Zoom™ is a trademark and logo of Abdo Consulting Group, Inc.

Printed in the United States of America, North Mankato, Minnesota
042017
092017

Cover Photo: Connie Barr/Shutterstock Images
Interior Photos: Charles Brutlag/Shutterstock Images, 1; Monicas Vault/iStockphoto, 4–5; Bonnie Taylor Barry/ Shutterstock Images, 6–7; iStockphoto, 8, 9, 10–11, 12, 13, 17, 18–19; Red Line Editorial, 11, 20 (left), 20 (right), 21 (left), 21 (right); Janet Forjan/iStockphoto, 14; George Olsson/iStockphoto, 15; Jim DeLillo/iStockphoto, 16

Editor: Brienna Rossiter
Series Designer: Madeline Berger
Art Direction: Dorothy Toth

Publishers Cataloging-in-Publication Data
Names: Statts, Leo, author.
Title: Cardinals / by Leo Statts.
Description: Minneapolis, MN : Abdo Zoom, 2018. | Series: Backyard animals |
    Includes bibliographical references and index.
Identifiers: LCCN 2017931126 | ISBN 9781532120022 (lib. bdg.) |
    ISBN 9781614797135 (ebook) | ISBN 9781614797692 (Read-to-me ebook)
Subjects: LCSH: Northern cardinal --Juvenile literature. | Birds--Juvenile literature.
Classification: DDC 598.8--dc23
LC record available at http://lccn.loc.gov/2017931126

Table of Contents

Cardinals

Cardinals are songbirds.
Their song sounds
like a whistle.

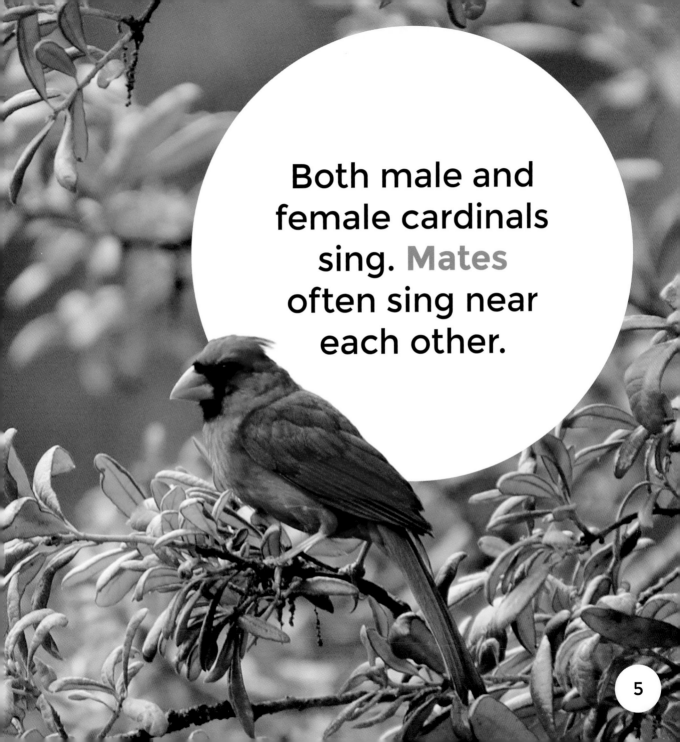

Both male and female cardinals sing. **Mates** often sing near each other.

Body

Male cardinals are red.
Females are brown.
Both have black feathers
around their beaks.

Cardinals have a **tuft** of feathers on their heads.

The tuft is called a crest. The feathers in a cardinal's crest stick up.

Habitat

Cardinals live in North America. They often live in warm places. But they can live in places with cold weather, too.

Where cardinals live

Some cardinals live in cities.

Others live in **rural** areas.

Cardinals eat seeds.

They eat berries and fruit. Sometimes they eat insects, too.

Life Cycle

Cardinals make nests.
Their nests are often
in bushes or trees.

A female cardinal lays three or four eggs in the nest. Chicks **hatch** from the eggs.

Cardinals care for the chicks. They bring them food. Chicks leave the nest after about 10 days.

Cardinals live an average of 15 years.

Average Weight

A cardinal is lighter than a deck of cards.

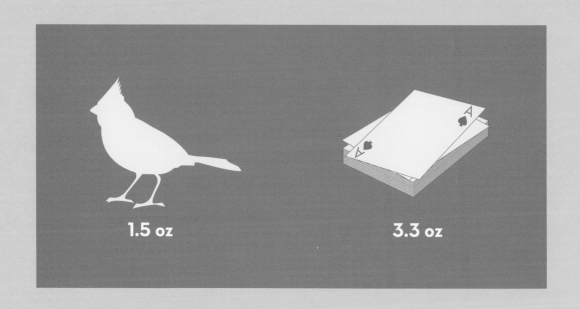

1.5 oz   3.3 oz

Average Length

A cardinal is not quite as long as a basketball.

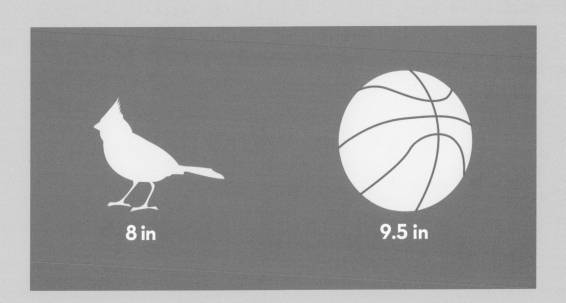

8 in   9.5 in

Glossary

beak - a hard mouthpart that sticks out.

hatch - to be born from an egg.

mates - a pair of animals who have joined together to have babies.

rural - open land away from towns and cities.

songbird - a bird with a musical song.

tuft - a small bunch of feathers or hair.

Booklinks

For more information on cardinals, please visit abdobooklinks.com

Zoom In on Animals!

Learn even more with the Abdo Zoom Animals database. Check out abdozoom.com for more information.

Index